Trump's Tricks
The Artful Use of Intimidation and Lies

Other Books by this Author

You're Not Nuts... You've Just Got Issues (2006)

For Parents & Teens: A Guide To Peaceful Coexistence (2007)

Them There Guys: An E-pistolary Odyssey (Gribin & Finkelstein, 2010)

Selfonomics: How Broadly-Defined Self-Interest Explains Everything (2013)

Road Trip: Europe 1967 (2014)

The Legacy Book: a guided autobiography (2016)

Doo-Wop: The Forgotten Third of Rock & Roll (Gribin & Schiff, 1992)

The Complete Book of Doo-Wop (Gribin & Schiff, 2000. Reissued 2009)

Who Sang Our Songs? (Friedman & Gribin, 2005)

The Encyclopedia Of Early American Vocal Groups: 100 Years Of Harmony - 1850-1950 (Friedman & Gribin, 2013)

The Top 1000 Doo-Wop Songs: Collector's Edition (Gribin & Schiff, 2014)

Doo-WopCentrism: The Top 2000 Doo-Wop Songs (2016)

Trump's Tricks
The Artful Use of Intimidation and Lies

Anthony J. Gribin, Ph.D.

ttgPress
2016

Trump's Tricks

The Artful Use of Intimidation and Lies

All Rights Reserved

Copyright © 2016 by Anthony J. Gribin, Ph.D.

All rights reserved. This book or any portion thereof may not be reproduced or used in any manner whatsoever without the express written permission of the publisher except for the use of brief quotations in a book review or scholarly journal.

ISBN-13: 978-0-9827376-8-2

ttgPress

Dedication

To Them There Guys (you know who you are) who stimulated my thought on this subject, despite your inane blathering.

Contents

Foreword

Introduction

Chapter 1:   Did You Hear What He Said?

Chapter 2:   I Heard It Through The Grapevine…

Chapter 3:   Blaming Everyone Else

Chapter 4:   Everyone Wants to Eat Our Lunch (xenophobia pays)

Chapter 5:   The Worst Incompetent Losers…

Chapter 6:   Convenient Truths (Uber-Pandering)

Chapter 7:   Convenient Untruths (Lies)

Chapter 8:   Projection

Chapter 9:   Business Tactics

Chapter 10:   Birds of a Feather

Chapter 11:   Nicknames

Chapter 12:   Convenient Fantasies (Policies?)

Chapter 13:   The Intimidator

Chapter 14:   This Ain't Beanbag

Afterword

Foreword

  This book almost ended about five times. The initial goal of this project was to gather a series of "data points" that described the verbal and behavioral tactics used by Donald Trump in his quest for the nomination and his subsequent campaign for President. The next step was to put them into somewhat distinct categories for the reader to peruse and evaluate.

  Following Donald's activities at his rallies, noticing his tweets, and monitoring what was written and said about him on a daily basis by the various media, kept providing me with more data points. I'd end up saying to myself, "I can't leave this stuff out. It's too good an example of _____." So I kept going…

  …And would've kept going if another motive wasn't in play; namely, the desire to get this out to the public while it was still relevant. The lag time between sending this to press and getting visible on Amazon and other selling venues, makes time somewhat of the essence since the Presidential election, as of the date below, is less than five months away. So, after including a few more interesting news items, I "put this to bed" on…

        June 15, 2016

        Anthony J. Gribin, Ph.D.

Introduction

A psychologist looks at the world differently than politicians or the news media. Personally, I'm searching for the motivations behind peoples thoughts and behaviors using common sense guided by experience and objectivity. What I look for are "data points" in behavior or speech that can be linked together to form a consistent pattern. For example, if a person has the tendency to be very critical of others, they are likely to leave a trail of contentious relationships scattered throughout their lives; with family, friends and coworkers. Once this type of repetitive theme is isolated and accepted by the patient (assuming it is accurate), change is possible.

The same strategy can work to define politicians. I can offer three examples: Mitt Romney from 2012, Chris Christie from 2013 and Hillary Clinton currently.

When Romney ran for President in 2012, he made numerous statements that attracted the attention of the media, especially left-leaning media. His (paraphrased) comments such as, "I only made $250,000 from my book," "I'll bet you $10,000" to rival Rick Perry, "My wife has two Cadillac Escalades," "My house in California has an elevator for cars," "I don't have to worry about the 47% of the people who will vote for the President" and, of course, the discovery that as a youth he was the ringleader of a group of boys at an exclusive prep school that bullied another student and took a scissors to his long hair. It would not be unreasonable for one to induce from these behaviors that Romney was out of touch with the common man.

Similarly, Chris Christie's behavior indicates a person who is comfortable being a bully. Kate Zernike's article in the New York Times[1] from December 2013, describes situations where people in power lost their jobs, their police escort, their funding, all for having crossed Christie in some minor way or even just disagreed with him.

In late October, 2014, he told a protester, "Sit down and shut up!" Not that he was wrong in *what* he said. But the way he said it and his choice of words and vehemence indicated his style. And of course, there is "Bridgegate" scandal, in which traffic jams were created in retribution for not supporting Christie's reelection, got national attention. Although it may be that Christie did not order the traffic jam, the cultural climate around him allowed others to do it.

Hillary comes off, at least in public, as quite competent and dedicated but lacking in warmth. Republicans have also labeled her as "untrustworthy,"[2] citing the e-mail server scandal, Whitewater and Benghazi. My guess is that she is seen as unlikeable because of the lack of warmth in combination of the strength of her assertions which, in our society, is not appreciated in a woman. Carly Fiorina, Christine Whitman and Condoleezza Rice suffered from the same fate. Angela Merkl, Margaret Thatcher and Golda Meir would have gone nowhere in American politics for the same reasons. The type of woman who is appealing has to be non-threatening or goofy, like Sarah Palin. The net-net is that Clinton's rep is that of a competent and dedicated public servant who is not particularly likable and is known to cut corners and

---

[1] Zernike, Kate. "Stories Add Up As Bully Image Trails Christie." New York Times, 12/24/13.

[2] Donald prefers the word "crooked."

shade the truth.

Data points for "The Donald" paint a different picture. His behavior and personality have been well documented. A glance at Amazon's book department offers well over a dozen biographical and/or diagnostic works on him, most (but not all) of which are, on balance, unflattering. The consensus seems to be that Donald fits the description of something that mental health professionals term "narcissistic personality disorder," as described in the DSM-5.[3] Here are the symptoms, as outlined by the Mayo Clinic[4]. Let the reader judge for him or herself whether Donald meets the criteria.

> Having an exaggerated sense of self-importance;
>
> Expecting to be recognized as superior even without achievements that warrant it;
>
> Exaggerating your achievements and talents;
>
> Being preoccupied with fantasies about success, power, brilliance, beauty or the perfect mate;
>
> Believing that you are superior and can only be understood by or associate with equally special people;
>
> Requiring constant admiration;
>
> Having a sense of entitlement;

---

[3] Diagnostic and Statistical Manual for Mental Disorders, 5th edition.

[4] Mayo Clinic Staff. "Diseases and Conditions: Narcissistic Personality Disorder." mayoclinic.com.

Expecting special favors and unquestioning compliance with your expectations;

Taking advantage of others to get what you want;

Having an inability or unwillingness to recognize the needs and feelings of others;

Being envious of others and believing others envy you;

Behaving in an arrogant or haughty manner.

The cause of narcissistic personality disorder is attributed to a combination of biogenetics and the environment, which basically means nothing (or everything). A person who exhibits these traits is likely to have a hard time in life. It may be very difficult for this person to work for someone else since they are likely to think that they know better and are smarter than those who supervise them. If they are extremely bright or knowledgable about their task they may be tolerated within a company as an eccentric, but if they bring only average skills to the table they will often be easy to terminate because of their superior attitude. They don't "play well in the sandbox."

Socially they will have few friends, from whom they demand total loyalty and admiration. They will push everyone else away, for most people don't like and won't tolerate "friends" that look down on them, are hostile and critical, and brag about their own accomplishments or possessions. They will think they are better than everyone else and will only want to associate with good looking, wealthy and successful people. Many who are diagnosed with NPD will lead unhappy lives, rejecting others and in turn being often rejected. Unhappy, that is, unless they are born rich or extremely good-looking.

When one is born into wealth, it is easy to grow into a sense of entitlement. You go to the best schools, you meet other scions of people with means, you make connections. But not everyone growing up in these circumstances needs to compete and win all the time. Aggressiveness is what set Donald apart from other rich kids. If one is willing to compete at anything and one has talents, which Donald certainly has (good looks, intelligence, athleticism) you often win. Winning feels good and you discover that if you are aggressive enough, you can intimidate people, be they classmates and girls, or later business competitors and girlfriends. Donald, without his money and intelligence, might've turned into a sour older man who couldn't hold a job and had trouble making his alimony and child support payments.[5] With his wile and his access to huge sums of money and people, he could conquer the world. Almost.

Most people would envy his life and lifestyle. But there have been bumps in the road. His business have filed for bankruptcy four times. He was married to his first wife, Ivana for 15 years. He was only 2 years older than she. His second marriage to Marla, 17 years his junior, lasted six years. Melania, his current wife, is 23 years his junior and they've been married for 11 years. His fortunes, literally and figuratively, have waxed and waned. All his wives are/were beautiful but it is open to question if these types of women, two of three being significantly younger, would've been attracted to Donald sans the fortune.

Donald always seemed to be looking for the next deal, involving buildings, golf courses, casinos or licensing

---

[5] Phil, a close friend suggested that he might have ended up as a used car salesman, married to a hooker and living in Vegas.

his name to neckties, steaks, planes or water. He developed and starred in a reality TV show from 2004 to the present called, "The Apprentice." Everyone knows his famous tag line at the end of the show, "You're Fired."

When you're on top of the world, or think you are, what do you do next? Where can you find a bigger arena than the New York metropolitan area real estate market or a successful TV show? National politics will do the job.

Donald doesn't do things in a small way. For a narcissist, things can't be incremental. If a person is really interested in *actual* public service, an earlier and more modest start would be the chosen path. Donald didn't choose to run for Congress, either for a House or Senate seat, or even to run for mayor or governor of New York. No halfway measures for Donald… the Presidency or bust.

Donald talked about running for President in 1988 and made a short lived run for the Reform Party in 2000. He also said he was considering a run in 2004, 2008 and 2012 before actually going for it in 2016. In passing, and at different times, he said that George Bush, Jimmy Carter and Barack Obama was the worst President ever.[6]

Up until his current run for President, Donald has basically been a businessman, who occasionally has voiced opinions on public and political issues. A look at the books he has written, with or without a co-author, include, The Art Of The Deal, Surviving At The Top, The Art Of The Comeback, How To Get Rich and Think Big and Kick Ass In Business And In Life. These titles tell you much about Donald; the way he thinks and the way he does business.

Does his style translate to the political sphere? I think many people might agree that it's not a natural fit. In his businesses, Donald is the boss; the decider. If he tries to

---

[6] Knoblauch, Max & Dailed, Colin. "All the times Donald Trump has pretended to run for president." mashable.com, 6/16/15.

make a deal with another guy and the guy doesn't give him what he wants, he can just walk away. There are plenty of other fish in the sea. And if he offends the other guy, does it really matter? The next guy down the line that fills his needs will be his business partner and best friend. The rest just don't matter.

Donald is also quite willing to use every legal trick in the book to get what he wants. He has filed for protection under the bankruptcy laws. He uses the court system when he feels it's necessary. He has been involved in approximately 3500 lawsuits over the last thirty years, around 1900 of which have been as plaintiff, 1450 as defendant and the rest fall in the category of "other." "The legal actions provide clues to the leadership style the billionaire businessman would bring to bear as commander in chief. He sometimes responds to even small disputes with overwhelming legal force. He doesn't hesitate to deploy his wealth and legal firepower against adversaries with limited resources, such as homeowners. He sometimes refuses to pay real estate brokers, lawyers and other vendors."[7]

Further, "The [lawsuits] in total paint a portrait of Trump's sprawling organization frequently failing to pay small businesses and individuals, then sometimes tying them up in court and other negotiations for years. In some cases, the Trump teams financially overpower and outlast much smaller opponents, draining their resources. Some just give up the fight, or settle for less; some have ended up in bankruptcy or out of business altogether."[8]

Trump and his daughter Ivanka, in an interview with USA TODAY, shrugged off the lawsuits and other claims of

---

[7] Penzenstadler, Nick & Page, Susan. "Exclusive: Trump's 3,500 lawsuits unprecedented for a presidential nominee." USA Today, 6/2/16.

[8] ibid

non-payment. If a company or worker he hires isn't paid fully, the Trumps said, "It's because The Trump Organization was unhappy with the work."[9]

And then of course, there are his tax returns that he won't release for reasons which don't hold water. The odds are he's doing nothing illegal, but that they would reveal something that he would prefer to keep under wraps.

So Donald is a man who, with few or no more worlds to conquer in the realm of business or entertainment, has sought to make his mark on the national and world stage, bringing with him a personal style that is foreign to politics as we know it, at least here in America. Further, the style that is Donald is comprised of autocratic, contentious and intolerant speech and behavior. And it's worked well for him.

But how does he do it? Since no politician has gone where Donald has gone, he brings a whole new set of strategies to the national scene. Some of them have been tried before, but Donald has used them on steroids. And some are novel to American politics. Whatever they are, not one of the 16 or so other Republican candidates had an answer to his style and bit the dust, one by one. He's the last one standing.

Most of the strategies make one suspend belief. They seem off the wall at first. Some of them are likely to be natural extensions of his way of doing business which include autocracy, contentiousness and intolerance. Others, it seems, were invented by Donald to adapt to the his new field of play; the national political scene. Together, they are "Trump's Tricks."

---

[9] Reilly, Steve. "USA TODAY exclusive: Hundreds allege Donald Trump doesn't pay his bills." usatoday.com, 6/9/16.

Chapter 1: Did You Hear What He Said?

Donald has been called a marketing genius. When he started his campaign, it was against a background of a man who had "considered" or threatened running for President at least four times before. He was known as the rich guy who developed and starred in a successful TV show. He was already an attraction in himself, and had enormous name recognition, but no political chops.

When the debates began in August, 2015 there were 17 candidates[10]; so many that they were divided into two groups of ten and seven. The top ten in the polls appeared in prime time, the rest were at the "kiddy table," and their debate appeared on television at an earlier time.

How could Donald stand out against the crowd? By saying outrageous things, of course. He got into arguments with two of the moderators, Chris Wallace and Megyn Kelly, mocked Jeb Bush for equating immigration with an act of love, and attacked the Mexican government for sending criminals and rapists across the border.

Three things ensued. First, Donald had tapped into a fairly large cohort of people who were anti-immigration and anti-immigrant. They loved it. Second, by saying outrageous things including the "….blood coming out of her wherever," about Megyn Kelly he became an attention magnet, from lovers and haters alike. The next morning everyone at work was saying, "Did you hear what he said?" Remember, 24 million people watched that first debate. Though most didn't yet think of him as a serious candidate,

---

[10] Observant readers and fans of "The Apprentice" might note that the show usually started with between 16 and 18 contestants so in a way, Donald was participating in his own real life season of his show. A better name for this would've been, however, "Survivor."

he sure piqued peoples interest, even if it involved schadenfreude, to get fun out of watching others squirm.

The third thing that happened was that the tendency to hurl these off the cuff insults, which came quite naturally to him, was reinforced by the next set of polls. He was steeled by his own success, and had no reason to turn back.

The marketing genius then took over. Using twitter, a field of play that Donald was quite comfortable with but was virtually unknown to the other candidates, and calls into news shows, Donald started to own the news cycles. If he tweeted something outrageous about another candidate, the media were quick to pick it up and call-ins were received gladly and with deference. After all, each network wanted his attention since it drove ratings.

Another benefit of machine gun insults is that it is very hard to focus on *one* particular insult when the next day there was another, and then another. Yesterday's insult becomes old news and listeners don't even pay attention to the content of the message or the victim of the assault. There's always a "victim du jour." And listeners become desensitized to what comes out of Donald's mouth; it's nothing new any more. We've come to expect it from him.

One by one, the other "contestants" dropped out, being defeated by Donald in debates (according to the voters, not necessarily the media), in tweet-wars, in media attention, and eventually in the ballot boxes. In debates, anyone who went after him or was critical was hit back twice as hard.

In the media, if someone gave Donald a hard time he'd excoriate you; witness Megyn Kelly, Jorge Ramos (Telemundo's most famous reporter who was kicked out of a Trump Q. and A.) and more recently Jim Acosta of CNN who was called "a real beauty" and Tom Llamas of ABC who was called "a sleaze." There is little motivation, either on the part of political rivals, media outlets or individual reporters to stand up to him. In effect, it's divide and conquer.

Chapter 2: I Heard It Through The Grapevine

Most of us are taught that it's not nice to say something bad about someone else. If I say something nasty about Ralph to Jim, Jim may figure that I'll say something bad about him to Ralph when his back is turned. But what if I say to Jim, "You know, I've heard people saying that Ralph is a liar." Or, "someone close to Ralph told me that he lies like crazy, so be careful when you deal with him." In these situations, I'm kind of doing Jim a favor, cluing him in about Ralph, but the information is not coming from me. I'm just being a good friend. By not being the source of the bad news, I can't be seen as the trash talker or the bad guy. And unless I'm willing to reveal my source, which is highly unlikely, especially if I made up the story, I can't be held accountable.

Or how about if I say, "Hey Ken, I heard down at the club that your wife has been running around on you! I don't know anything myself, but if it's true you've got to do something. You're going to look like a fool…" If Ken asks me to reveal my source I take umbrage in not really knowing, having just overheard a conversation. Or I can say I'm sworn to secrecy. I only told you because I like you and don't want you to look like a fool.

Everyone knows that Donald Trump was vocal in espousing the idea that Barack Obama was not an American citizen. No one accuses him of starting the rumor, but he was certainly its most avid advocate. "An 'extremely credible source' has called my office and told me that

Barack Obama's birth certificate is a fraud."[11] He said he had even sent investigators to Hawaii to determine the truth. Now we know if they had found anything positive we would've been told, so we have to assume that either (a) they found nothing and he didn't want to admit it or (b) he flat out lied about sending investigators.

Unfortunately when Donald makes those kind of assertions, uninformed people are not going to challenge him and ask the source of the information or, perhaps more importantly, ask why, as an educated and supposedly responsible adult, you don't check your sources and have proof before making such a serious claim?

What makes this kind of association so nefarious is that society is changing in a way to make each of us into an echo chamber. Frank Bruni calls it the "Facebook Effect."[12] We seek information that is consistent with what we believe and dismiss information that disagrees with our views. For example, if a person doesn't like Obama, they will read posts that attack him, take the information within the post as gospel, and be reinforced in their beliefs. Before the Internet, more extreme views were out there, but couldn't be spread virally since there was no medium for that kind of instant and unchecked proliferation. Facebook and other internet platforms gives any extremist the same clout as anyone else, making it easy to spread hatred.

Then there was the way he brought up and dwelt on the subject of Ted Cruz's citizenship. Cruz was targeted because he was Donald's closest rival in the polls and delegate count. "I'd hate to see something like that get in

---

[11] Marie-Claire magazine, May 4, 2016. http://www.marieclaire.co.uk/blogs/550112/donald-trump-quotes.html#yWAf1ip3D0y8Hr0H.99

[12] Bruni, Frank. "How Facebook Warps Our Worlds." Op-Ed, New York Times, 5/21/16.

his way," Trump said.[13] "But a lot of people are talking about it and I know that even some states are looking at it very strongly, the fact that he was born in Canada and he has had a double passport."[14] Donald never mentioned who the "people" were who were talking about it or the "states that are looking at it very strongly." In fact, the rumor, which Trump started, was debunked quickly and often by all media, but the seed had been planted. Trump tweeted: "Ted Cruz was born in Canada and was a Canadian citizen until 15 months ago. Lawsuits have just been filed with more to follow. I told you so."[15] At some point he even said that Cruz was an "anchor baby."

Cruz tried to turn the tables on Donald, using humor to do so, but Donald changed the subject quickly (another specialty). Cruz argued that if you take an extreme position on birtherism that Donald wouldn't be a citizen because both of his parents were not born in the U.S. (his mother was born in Scotland). When Donald said, "I was born here… big difference," Cruz quipped, "I'm not going to use your mother's birth against you." To which Donald responded with a non-sequitur, "In Iowa now, as you know, Ted, in the last three polls I'm beating you."[16] Take that, Ted!

Donald also went after Cruz' father Rafael, quoting a debunked story in the National Enquirer: "And, you know, [Cruz'] father was with Lee Harvey Oswald prior to

---

[13] Of course you would, Donald.

[14] Taken from an article by: Epps, Garrett. "Ted Cruz Is a Natural-Born Citizen" The Atlantic, 1/14/16.

[15] From Twitter, 1/16/16.

[16] Taken from an article by: Cooper, Allen. "Cruz turns tables on Trump with citizenship question." U.S.A. Today, 1/15/16.

Oswald's being — you know, shot. I mean, the whole thing is ridiculous. What is this, right, prior to his being shot, and nobody brings it up. They don't even talk about that. That was reported and nobody talks about it. But I think it's horrible." This time he didn't "hear" someone talking about the elder Cruz, but he supposedly read the article and assumed it was true, although I don't think any sentient human being thinks he really assumed it was actually true.

Last, Donald has come close to implying that one or both Clintons are guilty of murder. One issue on Trump's radar is the 1993 death of [Vince] Foster, which has been ruled a suicide by law enforcement officials and a subsequent federal investigation. But some voices on the far right have long argued that the Clintons may have been involved in a conspiracy that led to Foster's death. When asked in an interview last week about the Foster case, Trump dealt with it as he has with many edgy topics — raising doubts about the official version of events even as he says he does not plan to talk about it on the campaign trail. He called theories of possible foul play 'very serious' and the circumstances of Foster's death *very fishy*. 'He had intimate knowledge of what was going on,' Trump said, speaking of Foster's relationship with the Clintons at the time. 'He knew everything that was going on and then all of a sudden he committed suicide.'"[17]

"Indeed, this is exactly Trump's M.O. with literally every conspiracy theory, including the especially insane one that Ted Cruz's father was involved in JFK's assassination, is to say, 'Hey, I'm just bringing up concerns other people

---

[17] Wolf, Leon H. "Called it: Trump Implies that Hillary Clinton Killed Vince Foster." Red State (newsletter), 5/23/16.

have.'"[18] Yes, Donald, other people have those concerns. And many of them are locked away somewhere.

For those who have had or are interested in the subject of formal logic, Donald is a walking treasure trove of logical fallacies. For example, "Apophasis is a rhetorical device wherein the speaker or writer brings up a subject by either denying it, or denying that it should be brought up. Accordingly, it can be seen as a rhetorical relative of irony."[19] Donald used this beauty when he said he wouldn't talk about Vince Foster's death as he was in the process of talking about Vince Foster's death.

"Ad hominem" attacks just seem to roll off Donald's tongue. In general, ad hominem means that he attacks the *character* of another person (think Clinton, Obama), rather than address the *subject matter* under consideration.[20] In other words, when Donald can't rebut what another person is saying, he calls them a name. See, politics is easy!

---

[18] ibid

[19] wikipedia

[20] wikipedia: Abusive *ad hominem* usually involves attacking the traits of an opponent as a means to invalidate their argument(s). Equating someone's character with the soundness of their argument is a logical fallacy.

Chapter 3: Blaming Everyone Else

When Republican centrists were trying to figure out a way to deny Donald the nomination if he didn't get to the required delegate count of 1237 (in the beginning of 2016), Donald blamed the system. "Our Republican system is absolutely rigged. It's a phony deal," he said, accusing party leaders of maneuvering to cut his supporters out of the process. "They wanted to keep people out. This is a dirty trick."[21] In a way he was correct (occasionally paranoids are correct that people are out to get them), but instead of looking inward for having attitudes and policies that were anathema to the mainstream or realizing that his organization was not up to speed, he blamed the system. "'If Trump can't win something, he'll always say it's someone else's fault,' said Stuart Stevens, a Republican strategist who has advised several presidential candidates, most recently Mitt Romney in 2012."[22]

When responding to those questioning outbreaks of violence at his rallies, Donald would not accept any responsibility, saying that those who start trouble were sent by the other side, his enemies. He then switched gears. "The reason there's tension at my rallies is that these people are sick and tired of this country being run by incompetent people that don't know what they're doing on trade deals."[23] *Deny, distract and misdirect*, and at the time, no one calls

---

[21] Taken from an article by: Peters, Jeremy W. & Martin, Jonathan. New York Times, 4/12/16.

[22] ibid

[23] Taken from an article by: Chris Cillizza. "Donald Trump can't keep blaming other people for the anger of his campaign." The Fix, Washington Post, 3/13/16.

him on it. When someone does, it's a member of the media who, of course, is biased against him.

Donald either doesn't see, more likely sees but doesn't care, because it's working for him. His tough talk that includes violent phrases such as "get 'im outta here" or "knock the crap out of them" gives license to those attending his rallies to act out with angry talk or physical violence. To Donald, this indirect incitement to violence doesn't count. It would only be bad if he slugged someone.

It is obvious now, in 2016, that we should not have gone into Iraq in 2003. Many people say that we should have been more aggressive in Syria which may have prevented so many deaths and so much destruction. (Others believe that had we backed one faction in Syria, it would've created just as much chaos.) Libya is arguably in more of a mess than when Qaddafi was in charge. More people are out of work and can't find jobs. The middle class is being hollowed out. According to Donald, everything that went wrong is Obama's or Clinton's fault and that he, Donald, did know or would've known the right thing to do.

Donald said he would not have gone into Iraq. Nope. "Donald Trump has repeated throughout his presidential campaign that he opposed the Iraq war *before* the March 19, 2003 invasion, often taking credit for his judgement and vision — claiming he knew it would destabilize the Middle East. On Feb. 13, in the most recent debate, Trump said: 'I said it loud and clear, "You'll destabilize the Middle East."' In the Sept. 16, 2015 debate, Trump claimed that he 'fought very, very hard against us ... going into Iraq,' saying he could provide '25 different stories' to prove his opposition.'"

"Trump has even said that he was 'visited by people from the White House' in attempt to silence him, because, he said, he was getting 'a disproportionate amount of publicity' for his opposition to the war."[24]

Oops! This is basically a series of lies. Interviewed on Howard Stern's radio show, Trump said, "Yeah, I guess," when asked whether we should go into Iraq. Not really a big deal, but most important is that there is *no evidence whatsoever that he opposed the war before its start*. And Donald, who said he could provide 25 stories to corroborate what he said has not even come up with one, even knowing that if he did it would certainly give him more credibility.

On Libya, Donald said he was against going in and destabilizing the country. Not bad, but not true, either. In February, 2011, BuzzFeed investigated this claim. Trump was quoted as saying, ""You talk about things that have happened in history; this could be one of the worst,' he said. 'Now we should go in, we should stop this guy, which would be very easy and very quick. We could do it surgically, stop him from doing it, and save these lives. This is absolutely nuts. We don't want to get involved and you're gonna end up with something like you've never seen before.'" The attack on Libya began a month after he said this, in March 2011.

And, Trump said the people would take over from Qaddafi eventually and then "they should pay us back out of appreciation."[25] Again, it would be nice of it were true, but Donald gave us another pack of lies.

Of course, Donald has a long history on blaming everything on President Obama. Here are a series of tweets

---

[24] Kiely, Eugene. "Donald Trump and the Iraq War: A timeline of Trump statements about the Iraq war, before and after it started, from September 2002 to December 2003." FactCheck.org, 2/19/16.

[25] Kaczinski, Andrew & Massie, Christopher. "Trump Claims He Didn't Support Libya Intervention — But He Did, On Video." BuzzFeed News, 2/25/16.

by Donald reported by Tim Herrera of the Washington Post[26] that led the author to conclude that Donald lives in "a world of his own."

"Ebola has been confirmed in N.Y.C., with officials frantically trying to find all of the people and things he had contact with. Obama's fault"

"Russia beat the United States in the Olympics- another Obama embarrassment! Isn't it time that we turn things around and start kicking ass?"

"Congratulations to Obama on building a strong economy. There are 49,500,000 people on food stamps. A historic record!"

After Hurricane Sandy: "How about President Obama fixing the gasoline situation instead of taking photo ops in the destruction."

One thing he didn't blame on Obama: "Stop congratulating Obama for killing Bin Laden. The Navy Seals killed Bin Laden."

Oh, and how can we forget, Donald blamed Hillary for Bill's sex scandals, blamed Clinton and Sanders supporters for disruptions that occurred at his rallies, said that Hillary's opposition to the Muslim ban led to incidents like the EgyptAir crash in May and the San Bernadino shootings, said Hillary started the "birther movement," sees Obama and Clinton as the reason for the existence of ISIS and the civil war in Syria, among other things.

---

[26] Herrera, Tim. "A brief history of Donald Trump blaming everything on President Obama." The Fix, Washington Post, 10/24/14.

Chapter 4: Everyone wants to eat our lunch (xenophobia pays)

Webster's defines "xenophobia" as "fear and hatred of strangers or foreigners or of anything that is strange or foreign." Other dictionaries preface that definition with "unreasonable." But unreasonable is a value judgment, so we'll leave that word off.

One of the first policy statements Donald made had to do with building a wall between our southern border and Mexico, and making Mexico pay for it. Trump's exact words on June 16, 2015 were, "When Mexico sends its people, they're not sending their best. They're not sending you. They're not sending you. They're sending people that have lots of problems, and they're bringing those problems with us. They're bringing drugs. They're bringing crime. They're rapists. And some, I assume, are good people."[27]

And then, on 12/7/15, he announced, "Donald J. Trump is calling for a total and complete shutdown of Muslims entering the United States until our country's representatives can figure out what is going on. According to Pew Research, among others, there is great hatred towards Americans by large segments of the Muslim population."[28]

While he was alienating both Hispanic and Muslim voters, under the surface, he was tapping into the fears and hatred of a part of the American populace. His support for a ban of all Muslims came soon after Paris was attacked on November 13th, 2015. He doubled down on this policy

---

[27] newsday.com staff. "Donald Trump controversial campaign quotes." Newsday, 5/10/16.

[28] ibid

after the massacre in Orlando, but doesn't seem to realize that this hair trigger reaction plays precisely into the goals of our enemies and alienates the very people who can help us solve the problem over time; namely moderate Muslims.

Further, he lies as suits his needs. "'[Hillary] wants to take away Americans' guns and then admit the very people who want to slaughter us,' Trump said."[29] He also said that the Orlando murderer was born in Afghanistan when he was actually, as Clinton later pointed out, born in Queens, not far from where Donald grew up.

His desire to deport eleven million Mexicans tapped into economic fears of many whose jobs have been lost. The majority of these lost jobs can be attributed not to immigrants, but to by automation, technology or globalization. Both of these "excommunications" garnered him much support from those who felt threatened by terrorism or economic rivalry, but earned him a reputation as an isolationist, a bigot and a hate monger. Appealing to the basest of interests in people seemed to be all in a day's work for Donald and one of his most effective "tricks."

And while he hasn't banned Chinese people or called for their deportation (yet), he sees them as taking advantage of us economically. "You see [devaluations] almost everywhere except for the United States," he said. "We do nothing about it. We just sit back and let everybody do it. And that's getting to be very dangerous…They're taking advantage of our country. We don't have strong leadership. We don't have strong economic leadership at all." On one hand, Trump ramped up his blame-China rhetoric, calling Beijing "the grandmaster of all" when it comes to currency manipulation and free trade cheating. At the same time, he

---

[29] Collinson, Stephen & Diamond, Jeremy. "Donald Trump stretches facts in fiery post-Orlando speech." cnn.com, 6/14/16.

said: "My relationships with China are fantastic. I have great relationships and business relationships with China. Even those people are saying they can't believe what they are getting away with… We can't let the world take advantage of us from an economic standpoint. And that's what they are doing," he contended, calling for a stop to efforts by other countries to "suck more blood out of the United States."[30]

No matter that the United States economy, though far from perfect, is in pretty good shape, especially when compared to other economies around the world. (Of course any admission by Donald that our economy wasn't being mismanaged would deprive him of spurious talking points.) The Eurozone is still working to get out of the global recession of 2007-8 and China's economy, while still robust, has hit some speed bumps and is slowing down. And it's a curious situation when someone who has gamed the system to his advantage with four bankruptcies and tax returns that are hiding something, sees a problem with other countries trying to maximize their own outcomes. Shouldn't what's good for the Donald be good for the rest of the world?

A complicating factor that works in Donald's favor is that racial and other forms of prejudice are very difficult to recognize, talk about and eliminate. Racial prejudice has been studied most thoroughly as regards African-Americans. Charles Blow, an Op-Ed columnist for the New York Times reported on polls and studies on the subject of races in response to then Attorney General Eric Holder's

---

[30] Belvedere, Matthew L. "Trump: US must stop China from eating our lunch." CNBC, 3/10/16.

assertion that we were "a nation of cowards" because we don't have open and honest discussions about race.[31]

Blow found that, "...twice as many blacks as whites thought racism was a big problem in this country, while twice as many whites as blacks thought that blacks had achieved racial equality." And, "...72 percent of whites thought that blacks overestimated the amount of discrimination against them, while 82 percent of blacks thought that whites underestimated the amount of discrimination against blacks."

Apparently, racial biases, for the most part, are unrecognized. Why this happens is a subject for another tome and time, but a superficial guess involves "garbage in, garbage out" thinking. And whatever concepts we walk around with *are* us. We don't often have a need or reason to question our beliefs.

Even if we can admit to ourselves that we have racial biases, we rarely display them in public. It's just not "politically correct" or socially acceptable. Donald has made a point of railing against political correctness. There's no definitive reason why, but it strikes a chord with his large audiences. His xenophobic rants have given license to people who recognize their biases to feel like they are not pariahs, especially when your hero is saying it's okay and justified because "they're eating our lunch" or they are streaming across the border to kill us or rape our women. We are the victims, not them. And when you are surrounded by 10,000 others who are cheering because they feel liberated in the same way, it makes you feel good.

---

[31] Blow, Charles. "A Nation of Cowards?" New York Times Op-Ed, February 20, 2009.

Chapter 5: The Worst Incompetent Losers…

     Suppose you're playing basketball and your team loses. The guy you were guarding comes up to you and calls you "a loser," with no sign of a smile on his face. What would you do, or at least want to do to this guy? Perhaps kick him in the basketballs? Well, Donald has done this more than a few times. In the political world losers, according to Donald, include Barack Obama, Chuck Hagel, Jeb Bush, John McCain, David Cameron and Karl Rove. In the media, losers include Arianna Huffington, Bill Maher, Bill Moyers, George Will, Brian Williams, Charles Krauthammer, Chuck Todd and John Heilemann. Celebrity losers include Cher, Stevie Wonder, Jon Stewart, Jay Leno, Rihanna and Rosie O'Donnell.[32] Gotta say he's fair though… no party or network or medium is left out. It seems that the criterion for being called a loser by Donald amounts simply to disagreeing with or standing up to him.

     Or suppose you make a mistake on your job. Your boss comes over and calls you into her office. She doesn't just point out your error, but calls you "incompetent." How does that make you feel? How will that affect your morale and your loyalty to that boss and the company you work for? Donald does this on a regular basis too.[33] Apparently Barack Obama, Stuart Stevens (Romney's campaign manager), politicians, and, of course, the New York Times

---

[32] Gilmore, Scott. "The definitive list of every person Donald Trump has called a loser." MacLean's, 7/21/15.

[33] Lee, Jasmine C. & Quealy, Kevin. "The 223 People, Places and Things Donald Trump Has Insulted on Twitter: A Complete List." The Upshot, New York Times, 5/11/16.

are "incompetent." "Totally incompetent" was reserved for someone special: Hillary Clinton.

Donald even implied that his own campaign staff was "stupid." On a conference call to his surrogates (June 6, 2016) he instructed them to tear up a letter sent to them asking them to ignore questions on Trump University. Donald asked, "Are there any other stupid letters that were sent to you folks? That's one of the reasons I want to have this call, because you guys are getting sometimes stupid information from people that aren't so smart."[34]

Additionally, he has called Hillary and Bernie Sanders "crazy," not to mention Megyn Kelly and CNBC. Hillary is also "stupid" according to Donald, as are politicians, the Republican Party of Virginia, the New Hampshire Union Leader and the New York Times.

And suppose your boss says that not only are you incompetent, but you are the "worst" employee ever! That'll make you feel good, won't it? "Worsts" according to Donald include many of his former rivals for the nomination, including Ted Cruz, Marco Rubio, John Kasich and George Pataki, many minor Democrats such as Barack Obama, Bill and Hillary Clinton (separately), Bill De Blasio, and other public figures such as Mitt Romney and Anderson Cooper. We guess that Donald has very high standards. Here's a tweet that is a doozy: "Obama is, without question, the WORST EVER president. I predict he will now do something really bad and totally stupid to show manhood!"[35] After that statement, the reader may want to skip to the section on "projection."

Donald added a few descriptors during the week of May 30, 2016. A reporter was called a "sleaze" when he

---

[34] bloomberg.com, 6/7/16.

[35] Tweeted by Donald on 6/5/14.

questioned Donald's exaggeration of both timing and totals of the money he raised for veterans. Donald's defense was that he donated a million dollars, but the truth is he promised to do that months before and only wrote the check when egged on by the Washington Post. "When a reporter asked if a Trump presidency would take on a similar tone, the billionaire businessman responded, 'Yeah, it is going to be like this.' 'You think I'm going to change?' he said. 'I'm not going to change.'"[36]

Donald got indignant when he was questioned on his generosity. But here are some facts. Forbes magazine ranked Donald as the 121st richest person in America, with a net worth of 4.5 billion. According to an article in the NewsExaminer, Donald, over a period of 20 years, from 1990-2009, gave $3.7 million to his foundation, which then distributed it to various causes. While generous on the surface, it is less than one tenth of one percent of his current worth, spread over 20 years. In fact the article is entitled, "Donald Trump: The Least Charitable Billionaire In The World."[37]

Sadly, Donald gets away with this "trick," which is basically to call people names. Again, the veracity of the slur or the nickname is irrelevant, and is probably meant to say, "If you attack me (or even challenge me) I'll hit you back harder." Whether this strategy helps him in the long run remains to be seen because he seems to be making a lot of enemies and missing opportunity to make friends along the way.

---

[36] Krieg, Gregory. "WhenTrump hits back, he hits back hard." CNNpolitics, 6/1/16.

[37] Davis, Ben. "Donald Trump: The Least Charitable Billionaire In The World." NewsExaminer, September, 2016.

Chapter 6: Convenient Truths (Uber-Pandering)

Let's face it, all politicians pander. If a candidate is speaking in front of a particular audience, you can bet that he or she will embrace the causes of the group being addressed, and strictly avoid any views that they hold that run counter to the interests of the group. If they intended anything different they wouldn't be there. That's normal, and includes "code switching" where Barack Obama sounds "more black" when addressing black audiences, or when Donald or Joe Biden using more salty language while addressing blue collar audiences. But Donald takes pandering to a whole new level…

Pandering usually only reflects and supports the views of the audience. It usually doesn't egg them on to more extreme views. When talking to underemployed blue collar workers, who have lost jobs to automation, it would be "normal pandering" for a politician to say that he or she understands their plight and will work to retrain them or help them lift themselves out of the depths of poverty and despair. It's another thing to blame the Mexicans or the Chinese or the Democrats for their plight, and incite the audience to boo "the other." This is "uberpandering," defined as pandering plus incitement.

Donald panders in a more normal fashion when he says, "I love Mexicans! I love the Chinese! I love women! He surely touched many hearts when he said, "I love the poorly educated" in a victory speech in the Nevada caucuses in the beginning of February, 2016. Or how about, "I have a great relationship with blacks."[38] Does he really think that the objects of his affection are more drawn to him? In some cases, especially among the poorly educated, they probably are. To take a word from many of Donald's tweets, "sad."

Donald is different than other politicians in that he has no compunction about pandering to a particular group while in front of them, and then changing his tune as suits the occasion. In front of AIPAC (American Israel Public Affairs Committee), he said he was not going to pander to the crowd and then proceeded to pander to them, pledging his unwavering support for Israel. This is against a background of professing to want to stay neutral in the disagreement between the Israelis and the Palestinians.[39]

In front of many audiences he says he wants to increase taxes on the wealthy, including himself. When he put forth his proposal for a tax cut, however, it favored the rich more than the plans of any of the other Republican candidates. He said that people shouldn't "die in the streets" for want of health care and then, in the next breath (or next town) said the first thing he will do is abolish Obamacare. In a way, he's an equal opportunity panderer, no one being beyond his largesse. It is no doubt a large part of the reason why conservative Republicans fear that Donald is too liberal on too many issues. He's a "man for all seasons," pander-wise.

---

[38] Taken from Oslyn, Sam. "36 DONALD TRUMP QUOTES THAT PROVE HE CAN'T BE PRESIDENT." Press Room VIP, 7/7/15. The author goes on to add, "Unless the Blacks are a family of white people, we're not so sure."

[39] Chotiner, Isaac. "Trump Says He Won't Pander to AIPAC Before Pandering to AIPAC, Of Course." slate.com, 3/21/16.

Does Donald's approach to tell everyone he meets that he loves them actually work for him? He says he loves everybody in every state he campaigns in. He loves Mexicans, Muslims, China, vets, evangelicals, the poorly educated, protesters and even the New York Times.[40] And, of course, everyone loves him, including the Chinese, the Mexicans, Putin, the North Koreans and yes, women love him too!

Unfortunately, this in not necessarily borne out by polls. 87% of Hispanics disapprove of Donald,[41]/[42] as do 70% of women.[43] Plus Donald has about 10% support from African-Americans. "In short, there is absolutely no evidence that Donald Trump has strong support from any minority group in the United States. Ethnic minorities are strongly opposed to Donald Trump's presidential campaign. The Trump agenda of ethnic and religious and broad cultural hostility seems to have alienated almost everybody but heterosexual European-American Christian Republicans.[44]

Donald's view of loving everyone and being loved by everyone brings up certain questions, especially in light of the data. If you love every person in every group you talk to doesn't that water things down a bit? And perhaps mean that you don't love anyone (with the possible exception of

---

[40] Moos, Jeanne. From the Erin Burnett Show. CNN, 2/25/16.

[41] Dinan, Stephen. "Donald Trump Gets Crushed Among Hispanic Voters. Washington Times, 4/21/16.

[42] Fabiola, Santiago. "Donald Trump Says Hispanics Love Him. Survey says: Wrong! Miami Herald, 4/26/16.

[43] Gallup Daily Tracking. gallup.com, 4/21/16.

[44] Clifford, J. "Fact Check: Does Donald Trump Have Strong Minority Support?" Irregular Times, 12/31/15.

yourself)? And if you think everyone loves you, are you kind of "protesting too much?" That is, perhaps no one cares for you and you have to convince yourself. What is clear is that you are trying to deceive the people you're addressing and that maybe they don't believe you. It's time to turn to convenient UNtruths…

Chapter 7: Convenient Untruths (Lies)

How many times can a friend lie to you before you never trust him again? Though it probably depends on the strength and duration of the relationship, and the seriousness of the lie, my guess is not many. After you're sure you've been lied to once, there's always doubt in the back of your mind about the liar. (Similarly, if someone stole something from you, you'd never leave them alone in your house.) But what if the liar is so appealing and charismatic that you either overlook the lies or excuse them. Or there's always the possibility that you are too ignorant of the actual facts (not stupid) to know whether what's being told to you is the truth, or you simply don't care, believing in effect, that the end justifies the means. Enter Donald…

Who can forget Donald's assertion that he saw thousands of Arabs celebrating after the World Trade Center buildings came down? "…the folly of trying to fact-check Donald Trump. Even when confronted with contrary information — 'police say it didn't happen' — he insists that with his own eyes he saw 'thousands and thousands' of cheering Arabs in New Jersey celebrating as the World Trade Center collapsed during the Sept. 11 attacks."[45] Donald amended the story several times, starting at "I watched it in Jersey City," then "I saw it on TV" and, I guess conveniently, he chose not to say anything about this until roughly fourteen years after it happened. He's either outright lying, has a faulty memory, is being willfully malicious or has serious psychological problems. Actually

---

[45] Kessler, Glenn. "Trump's outrageous claim that 'thousands' of New Jersey Muslims celebrated the 9/11 attacks." Fact Checker, Washington Post, 11/22/15.

let's give him credit… it could be a combination of any or all of these four explanations.

Note that Donald assumes what he has said is true and then expounds by saying something like "these people hate us." He asserted that Islam hates America and Americans in an interview with Anderson Cooper of CNN in early May of 2016. This is the basis of his demand that Muslims be banned from the United States.

There's also an assertion by Donald that Hillary Clinton wants to abolish the second amendment. It's no coincidence that he said this while speaking in front of the NRA, who endorsed his candidacy for President. Then, as he is wont to do, Donald assumed the truth of the lie he just made up and expanded it. "We're not going to let that happen," Trump said. "We're going to preserve it, we're going to cherish it."[46] (What Clinton has said is that she wants universal background checks and more stringent controls on firearms, but sees gun ownership as a right of citizenship.)

Then, going off on a tangent, he turned the topic to women. He stated that Clinton is telling "every woman that she doesn't have the right to defend herself" with a firearm. Extending again... "That is so unfair and that is so egregious and I'll tell you what, my poll numbers with women are starting to go up," he said. Beautifully crafted, even though none of what he said was true. Starts with a lie, indicates that he will stand up to his imaginary bogeyman (Clinton) and then show how women will be better off with him as President because his imaginary bogeyman is going to take guns away from imaginary women. Whew! That's good!

---

[46] Diamond, Jeremy. "Donald Trump goes after Hillary Clinton on guns." CNN Politics, 5/20/16.

Another interesting thing about Donald's lies is that he never admits to them. Never. If caught, he will say he didn't say what he said, he will change topics and go off on a tangent so as not to address the lie, he will reiterate the lie and maintain that he was correct in the first place or, an happened recently (in the "Case of the Mexican Judge") said his comments were misconstrued. Has the reader every met anyone who never thought they were wrong, never backed down from an obviously wrong, or never apologized for a lie? If so, what did you think of him or her? This is the person that has a shot to be our President.

Though we will revisit this topic later, isn't it interesting and noteworthy that no one, and we mean no one, ever calls him a liar. Or without calling *him* a liar, at least challenges what he has said, in effect, "That is a lie!"

Chapter 8: Projection

"Psychological projection is a theory in psychology in which humans defend themselves against their own unpleasant impulses by denying their existence while attributing them to others. For example, a person who is habitually rude may constantly accuse other people of being rude. It incorporates blame shifting."[47]

Commonly, "The angry person accuses someone else of being angry; a liar accuses others of lying; the cheater accuses others of cheating; the thief accuses others of stealing."[48]

Projection is not always pathological. In a way it is a natural consequence of each of us having our own beliefs and of believing, to some extent, that others think the way we do. If I love a song, I think that you do or at least should also, and may have trouble understanding why you don't care for it. How can you not? If I am a very critical person, I may think that others are thinking the same way and thus are critical as well. A person who is a "glass half-empty" type may have trouble understanding a person who sees the "glass half-full," and vice versa, most of the time. People who go out of their way for others, think that others should reciprocate, and end up being repeatedly disappointed.

When we (psychologists) talk about projection as a "psychological defense mechanism" however, we are talking about those who deny their own negative feelings but accuse others of the same feelings, thus "projecting" his/her own feelings onto others. A defense mechanism, to

---

[47] wikipedia

[48] Pliers, Bernard. "Psychology Of Hatred Part II: Projection & Projective Identification." Daily Kos, 5/12/13.

be classified as such has to be "unconscious," or not in a person's awareness. Enter Donald...

There are plenty of psychologists who are sure that Donald is a narcissist, or can be diagnosed with Narcissistic Personality Disorder (NPD).[49]/[50]/[51] There are also many biographies, actually too many to list, of the man, some authorized, some not. In this section the goal is to look at the way he projects bad feelings onto others. There's a question, however, if these projections are conscious or not. Does he really believe what he claims, or is he just exploiting a weakness that he sees in others?

Recently, attention has been paid to Donald's Trump University, since there are many accusations that it was a money maker that helped almost no one. "During a campaign stop in San Diego on Friday, presumptive GOP presidential nominee Donald Trump devoted a significant amount of time to attacking the federal judge overseeing the ongoing case against Trump University, suggesting the judge is a 'hater' who is biased against him. The case against the real estate mogul's now-defunct company, which has been accused of scamming students who were misled into paying money for insight from business experts they thought were hand-picked by Trump, is scheduled to go to trial in San Diego federal court shortly after the presidential election. According to his lawyer, Trump is planning on testifying. In what the Wall Street Journal characterized as an 'extended tirade,' Trump spent 12 minutes of his 58-

---

[49] Alford, Henry. "Is Donald Trump Actually a Narcissist? Therapists Weigh In!" Vanity Fair Psychological Profile, vanityfair.com, 11/11/15.

[50] Lancer, Darlene. "Donald Trump and the Narcissistic Illusion of Grandiosity." PsychCentral, 2015.

[51] Guarnizo, Fr. Marcel. "Trump Is Simply Not Well." townhall.com, 3/31/16.

minute speech focused on the case and the California judge who will hear it. 'I have a judge who is a hater of Donald Trump, a hater. He's a hater. His name is Gonzalo Curiel,' Trump told the crowd. 'I think Judge Curiel should be ashamed of himself.'"[52]

There's a punchline here. Donald, who has expressed his distaste for Mexican immigrants and insists he will build a wall at Mexico's expense, said that the judge was biased because he is of Mexican heritage.[53] It does sound like there is a "hater" in the mix, and it's unlikely to be that judge.

Then there's "Lyin' Ted." Here's the way, likely unplanned, that the nickname was born. "Cruz and Rubio had ganged up on Trump, accusing him of waffling on his tough talk on immigration. They specifically noted reports that Trump made off-the-record comments to The New York Times about immigration and questioned whether those comments would undercut his rhetoric.

Cruz said, "'That's why this New York Times tape is so troubling, because what's been reported is Donald told the editorial board of The New York Times, 'What I'm saying on immigration, I don't believe. I'm not going to build a wall, I'm not going to deport people,' this is all just rhetoric for the voters,' '…If he didn't say that, he has an easy solution — simply release the tape.'"

A few minutes later in the debate Donald responded, "'You're the lying guy up here. You're the one, you're the one,' Trump said. 'I've given my answer, Lying Ted. I've given my answer.' While Trump debuted the pejorative nickname for Cruz during a Super Tuesday rally, it's the

---

[52] Culp-Ressler, Tara. "Trump Attacks Judge Overseeing The Case Against His Fake University: 'He's A Hater.'" ThinkProgress.com, 5/28/16.

[53] He was born in Indiana, to parents of Mexican heritage.

first time he's used it on a national forum."[54] Considering that Donald makes up things as he goes along, this is, as they say, "rich."

If unconscious, Donald is using the defense mechanism of projection; that is, Donald lies, so others lie. If conscious, Donald is just looking for any word that will demean and/or embarrass another person. He calls someone a name and if he gets applause or laughs, he repeats it. (He repeats himself anyway, a special trope of his.) This is just evidence of a street fighter who will do or say anything to hurt his opponent. Nothing is off the table and the truth of the assertion is totally irrelevant.

And then there was the time when he accused Hillary of playing the "women's card," saying that it was the only thing she had going for her. She responded by saying, "If fighting for women's health care and paid family leave and equal pay, then deal me in!"[55] He then accused her of shouting implying that women should be more demure. Aside from the fact that women not shouting is ridiculous, have you ever heard Donald on the stump? That's all he does… yell and repeat himself (the only times that Donald is calm and collected is when he is calling in to news shows to talking heads that throw him softball questions). Incidentally, Bernie Sanders raises his voice on the stump, just like Donald and Clinton do. So much for equal rights. Guys can raise their voices; women, not so much. Again, a clear case of projection.

Another laugher involving projection is his assertion that Hillary was to blame for the birther movement. In an interview with CNN's Wolf Blitzer, he said "You know who

---

[54] Kamisar, Ben. "Trump digs at Cruz, calling him 'Lyin' Ted.'" the hill.com, 3/3/16.

[55] Clip from Morning Joe, "Trump: Clinton Shouted During Her Speech." 4/27/16

started the birther movement? You know who started it? Do you know who questioned his birth certificate, one of the first? Hillary Clinton. She's the one that started it. She brought it up years before it was brought up by me."[56] This is not only an example of an out and out lie, but a beautiful attempt at projection. Donald gets two points for that one.

The fear of every foreign country taking advantage of us, making fools of us and eating our lunch is also projection. Donald manipulates anything and everything he can, using lawsuits, denial of payments to creditors and filing bankruptcy (four times) to take advantage of anyone he does business with. This may be more unconscious and less an attempt to demean other countries since competing for money is what he lives for and by. And in the world of business at least, he is surely not the only one who cuts corners. The phrase "it takes one to know one" seems applicable here.

---

[56] Ye Hee Lee, Michelle. "Donald Trump's ridiculous claim that Hillary Clinton started the birther movement." Fact Checker, Washington Post, 5/6/16.

Chapter 9: Business Tactics

We're guessing Donald is a great businessman, although there are signs that all's not what it seems to be. He started his career by running his father's real estate business, worth around 200 million when he took over in 1974. He did grow net assets enormously while he was there for eight years, but let's face it, he didn't start in the mail room. And most people smart enough to get through Wharton with no college debt, who have the connections of Fred Trump and begin their careers in a fire-proof job, probably would've done okay also.[57] "Remember, too, that Mr. Trump is a clear case of someone born on third base who imagines that he hit a triple: He inherited a fortune, and it's far from clear that he has expanded that fortune any more than he would have if he had simply parked the money in an index fund."[58]

Along the way, he filed bankruptcy; not personal bankruptcy, but his businesses went bankrupt four times. Not once, but four times. Donald sees that as a tool to be used by astute business people that is entirely within the law, which is correct. But it is a tool that is available only to the more affluent. In other words you have to own a business to file bankruptcy for that business.

And when there is a filing, there are bills that are not being paid, which means someone further down the food chain is losing money. If a loan to a bank is not repaid, the bank loses money and the shareholders of that bank stock

---

[57] Sherman, Amy. "Did Donald Trump inherit $100 million?" Politifact Florida, 3/7/16.

[58] Krugman, Paul. "Trump's Delusions of Competence." New York Times, Op-Ed, 5/27/16.

lose money. Maybe they can afford it and it is a kind of "victimless crime," but someone is losing. The field on which Donald plays represents a zero-sum game. When one person wins, someone else loses.[59]

A recent article in the New York Times questions not only Donald's judgment, but his ability or willingness to tell the truth, and his ethics as well. Being well-known in real estate, Donald was able to raise money to build and open casinos, but at exorbitant interest rates. As a result, the nut that he carried made it likely that the casinos would fail. Between 1997 and 2002, when other casinos made a profit of 18%, Donald's casinos lost 1%. "…court records and security filings by The New York Times leaves little doubt that Mr. Trump's casino business was a protracted failure…"[60]

"During a decade when other casinos here thrived, Mr. Trump's lagged, posting huge losses year after year. Stock and bondholders lost more than $1.5 billion.… …All the while, Mr. Trump received copious amounts for himself, with the help of a compliant board. In one instance, The Times found, Mr. Trump pulled more than $1 million from his failing public company, describing the transaction in securities filings in ways that may have been illegal, according to legal experts."[61]

In spite of the evidence, Donald maintained that his casino businesses were a success, touting his own foresight in getting out at the right time. He did, but it was the right

---

[59] Stewart, Emily. "The Backstory on Donald Trump's Four Bankruptcies." theStreet.com, 9/15/15.

[60] Buettner, Russ & Bagli, Charles V. "How Donald Trump Bankrupted His Atlantic City Casinos, but Still Earned Millions." New York Times, 6/11/16.

[61] ibid

time for him only. Most investors lost money. "Atlantic City fueled a lot of growth for me," Mr. Trump said in an interview in May, summing up his 25-year history here. "The money I took out of there was incredible."[62] So not only was the judgment off in starting his casino businesses, but he was delusional or lied about how successful he was. Further, taking money out of a failing business seems tantamount to insider trading, where an owner of a stock, knowing that the business is in trouble, sells his shares before the news hits the market. He doesn't lose but everyone else does.

There's also his reluctance, rather refusal, to release his tax returns. Let's face it, if the returns showed that he was worth what he says he's worth ($10 billion), that he paid a reasonable amount of taxes (Mitt Romney paid 14%) and that he donated a reasonable amount to charity (Mitt Romney gave 14% to charity) we would've seen them already. It's obvious that he's got something to hide. My guess is that there's nothing illegal in what is in the tax returns, but that his schemes to avoid paying taxes would be an embarrassment to him, and/or perhaps counter his claim of the extent of his wealth.

"One of the many peculiar things about his run for the White House is that it rests heavily on his claims of being a masterful businessman, yet it's far from clear how good he really is at the 'art of the deal.' Independent estimates suggest that he's much less wealthy than he says he is, and probably has much lower income than he claims to have, too. But since he has broken with all precedents by refusing to release his tax returns, it's impossible to resolve

---

[62] ibid

such disputes. (And maybe that's why he won't release those returns.)"[63]

But let's overlook the six caveats (his head start, the bankruptcies, his ethics, his truth telling, his judgment and the tax returns) above. Donald plays hardball and is proud of it. It's his way or the highway. A long time ago, a forgotten client whose company did business with Trump got a phone call to the effect (paraphrased from memory), "You sent me a bill for $80,000. I'm sending you a check for $40,000. That's all you're getting. If you don't like it sue me…"

Apparently, this was not an anomaly. "At least 60 lawsuits, along with hundreds of liens, judgments, and other government filings reviewed by the USA TODAY NETWORK, document people who have accused Trump and his businesses of failing to pay them for their work. Among them: a dishwasher in Florida. A glass company in New Jersey. A carpet company. A plumber. Painters. Forty-eight waiters. Dozens of bartenders and other hourly workers at his resorts and clubs, coast to coast. Real estate brokers who sold his properties. And, ironically, several law firms that once represented him in these suits and others."[64]

It's easy for him to walk away from a business deal if he doesn't get the terms he wants. There are plenty of fish in the sea, so if he can't get concessions from one firm, he can find another that will take the deal. That's fine, but how do you do this internationally? If you play tough with China and they balk, do you walk away and deal with

---

[63] Krugman, Paul. op cit.

[64] Reilly, Steve. "USA TODAY exclusive: Hundreds allege Donald Trump doesn't pay his bills." usatoday.com, 6/9/16.

Russia? Is it okay to anger entire countries and populations?

And can you expect no repercussions from needing to win all the time? If you win all the time, someone else is losing all the time. And they probably won't like it. It's not like business where you don't care if nine out of ten businessmen dislike you because there's always a tenth guy who you can work with. Silly them, but countries generally think that their people and economies are just as important as yours. For example, if import tariffs are slapped on China, they will establish trading partners elsewhere. International deals have to be almost always win-win else there are significant and unpredictable negative consequences.

Further, diplomacy, in terms of the way you talk to people and the respect you show them and the way you follow an agreed-upon set of rules, determines whether you make friends or enemies. Donald, in his words and actions shows no sign that he will be able to even feign being diplomatic. He even laughs at the desire to be "PC" (politically correct). Let's take a look at the extent to which he has angered and scared other nations:

Mexico: "When Mexico sends its people," Trump said during his presidential announcement, "they're not sending the best. They're not sending you, they're sending people that have lots of problems and they're bringing those problems. They're bringing drugs, they're bringing crime. They're rapists and some, I assume, are good people, but I speak to border guards and they're telling us what we're getting."[65] Combined with Donald's promise to build a wall

---

[65] Kohn, Sally. "Trump's outrageous Mexico remarks." CNN Opinion, 6/18/15.

at our southern border and make Mexico pay for it, this is not likely to lead to good relations between the countries.

China: "After months of lamenting that 'we are being ripped so badly by China' in trade and that it is 'playing us like a fiddle' in dealing with North Korea, Donald Trump took his tough-on-China rhetoric to new extremes last week, declaring on Sunday, 'We can't continue to allow China to rape our country' with trade deficits. 'It's the greatest theft in the history of the world, the presumptive Republican nominee said."[66]

"Rarely has a candidate so relentlessly attacked a peaceful trade partner. Trump has accused China of manipulating its currency and stealing American jobs, and promised a 45 percent tariff on all Chinese goods—intended to devastate the country's export-driven economy."[67]

Donald's bravado in saying how he will deal with China is open to some question. He has done deals with Chinese billionaires and the results have been not overly successful, either seen from the outside or by Donald. He entered into a deal with two Chinese partners in 1994, the partners putting up cash (which baled out Donald who was in deep debt) in return for a majority stake in the investment. All made money on the deal, but the partners sold the property in 2005 without consulting Donald That is, according to Donald. His partners say they informed him.

"Instead of accepting his share of the proceeds, Mr. Trump sued his partners for 'staggering breach' of fiduciary duty in a lawsuit that demanded $1 billion in damages. Mr.

---

[66] Mak, Aaron. "Why China's Not Afraid of Donald J. Trump." Politico Magazine, 5/8/16.

[67] ibid

Lo, who felt that Mr. Trump should have been appreciative of the deal he had received, called the lawsuit 'a shock.'"[68] The lawsuit was a mixed blessing. Donald got to keep his original stake in the deal, but the stake was tied up for 30 years and he lost a relationship that had been very financially rewarding. Called into question is Donald's strategy of "my way or the highway." It just doesn't seem to work when the people he's dealing with are just as powerful as he.

Donald has even alienated Americans doing business in China. "Executives of American companies manufacturing in China are joining forces against Trump as the presumptive Republican Party nominee trudges towards the White House.'China and America are economically married, in that they that need each other, and Trump wants to cause conflict that can break this relationship,' said an executive for a $2 billion American appliance manufacturer based in China. The source did not want to use his name or have his company name made public. 'It would be a tragedy for both parties if Trump wins,' he said, adding he feared that a Trump government could put tariffs on his products that do not benefit from Chinese subsidies."[69]

Japan: "'You have so many countries already -- China, Pakistan, you have so many countries, Russia -- you have so many countries right now that have them [referring to nuclear bombs],' Trump said in a Milwaukee, Wisconsin town hall televised by CNN. 'Now, wouldn't you rather, in a

---

[68] Stockman, Farah & Bradshaw, Keith. "Donald Trump Soured on a Deal, and Hong Kong Partners Became Litigants." New York Times, 5/30/16.

[69] Rapoza, Kenneth. "American Executives In China Join Forces Against Trump." forbes.com, 6/1/16.

certain sense, have Japan have nuclear weapons when North Korea has nuclear weapons? ...Trump said that the United States spends too much money protecting countries like Japan and Saudi Arabia, but 'we can't afford to do it anymore.'"[70]

Great Britain: "[Donald] was asked about comments by British Prime Minister David Cameron, leader of the U.K.'s Conservative Party, who said that Trump's suggestion Muslims should be barred from the United States was 'divisive, stupid and wrong.' Trump told Good Morning Britain that 'it looks like we're not going to have a very good relationship,' if he were to win the presidential election in November."[71]

What it all means is that "my way or the highway" is not likely to work in his favor, or in America's favor in the international sphere. However, this "trick" does play to his base. Angering either the leaders, businessmen or populace of other countries is just likely to make it tougher on American businesses. As a matter of fact, countries are planning "just in case" scenarios to look out for their own interests in the event Donald comes out on top. A good summary of the situation was offered by Barbara Crossette at the end of an article for The Nation: "Benn Steil and Max Boot are conservative commentators, yet in a bruising article in *The Weekly Standard* on February 26 they jointly sounded a warning about the havoc in the world and the terrible destruction of US relations with allies and foes alike that would follow if Trump were elected and operated on

---

[70] Condon, Stephanie. "Donald Trump: Japan, South Korea might need nuclear weapons." CBS News Online, 3/29/16.

[71] Smith, Alexander. "Donald Trump to British PM David Cameron: 'I'm Not Stupid, OK?'" NBC News, 5/8/16.

his ill-thought-out threats. "Trump has already done considerable damage to America's reputation with his crude, bombastic and often ugly rhetoric," they wrote. "American standing, as measured in both 'soft power' and more traditional realpolitik terms, would suffer far more if he were to become commander in chief. A Trump presidency threatens the post-World War II liberal international order that American presidents of both parties have so laboriously built up—an order based on free trade and alliances with other democracies."[72]

    Can Donald reverse course or tone it down? Probably not, since the hardball way he does business is so much a part of who he is. Further, it is likely that even if were able to put on a veneer of civility and tone it down a few notches, that leaders of other countries would not trust his sudden shift.

---

[72] Crossette, Barbara. "Where Do the Presidential Candidates Stand on the United Nations?" the nation.com, 3/9/16.

Chapter 10: Birds of a Feather

They say you are judged by the company you keep. Well, if true, it doesn't say much for Donald. First, there's his bromance with Vladimir Putin. "Donald Trump on Friday praised Vladimir Putin and appeared to defend the autocratic Russian president when pressed about his alleged killing of journalists and political opponents critical of his rule. One day after Putin called Trump a 'bright and talented' and the 'absolute leader of the presidential race,' the Republican presidential front-runner returned the compliments, hailing Putin as a 'leader' and pointing to his high favorability numbers in Russia."[73] Putin, in case people haven't noticed has done everything he can to be aggressive wherever and whenever he has been able to, including forays into Georgia, Crimea and Ukraine, not to mention Syria and, indirectly through Iran, other mid-eastern nations.

In March, 2016 Donald hired Paul Manafort, who lobbied for Viktor Yanukovych, Putin's ally and Prime Minister of the Ukraine, who summarily left office as the result of what was termed the "Orange Revolution" in 2014. An old partner of Manafort, Roger Stone, has written hatchet job books on the Clintons which would be amusing if the subjects weren't serious. He wrote "The Clinton's War On Women" which is the basis of Donald Trump's attack on Hillary in the 2016 Presidential campaign, and "Jeb! and the Bush Crime Family," which is part of the

---

[73] Diamond, Jeremy. "Donald Trump lavishes praise on 'leader' Putin." CNN Politics at CNN.com, 12/18/15.

reason why no member of the Bush family has any use for Donald. He employed ghostwriters for both.[74]

Stone recounted that as a youngster rooting against Kennedy in 1960, he remembers "...going through the cafeteria line and telling every kid that Nixon was in favor of school on Saturdays...It was my first political trick".[75] It seems that he hasn't changed since. Donald, a bird-of-a-feather denied knowing anything about Stone's hatchet job on the Clintons. Denied it that is, after having mentioned and promoted it months before.[76]

And Stone, Donald's associate of 40 years, was banned from appearing on CNN after he tweeted about a female republican talking head, calling her an "entitled diva bitch," "borderline retarded," "dumber than dog shit" and said she reminded him of a "rabid pekinese." This is the kind of person that Donald keeps close to him. Along with Manafort, he's right up Donald's alley.

Then there are the people that jumped on board his bandwagon when it appeared that he was going to win the race for the nomination. The first two were Sarah Palin and Chris Christie. Oddly, Donald looked embarrassed while Palin gave her supportive speech (because she was talking nonsense) and Christie looked embarrassed behind Donald as he spoke (because Donald was speaking nonsense). Ben Carson jumped on board after being made fun of and called a pedophile by Donald. Then there were Rick Perry and Dan Quayle, men whose reputation falls short of being stellar.

---

[74] wikipedia

[75] wikipedia.

[76] Hananoki, Eric. "Donald Trump Lies About Relationship With Roger Stone."

Oh, and we forgot Dick Cheney, who defended waterboarding, which seems to just be a starting point for Donald. Now one could argue that Donald didn't mean what he said, but… "'"Look, we have to change our law on you know on the waterboarding thing, where they can chop off heads and drown people in cages and heavy steel cages and we can't waterboard. We have to change our laws and we have to be able to fight at least on almost equal basis. We have laws that we have to obey in terms of torture. They have no laws whatsoever they have to obey," Trump said."[77]

Although Donald was endorsed by David Duke, a former leader of the Ku Kux Klan, he didn't repudiate that endorsement until two days had passed and he was pressured to do so. He at first denied that he knew who Duke was, but it was quickly revealed that Donald had previously denounced him several times before. Why the lie, Donald?

If the people mentioned above are your cup of tea (Putin, Manafort, Stone, Yanukovych, Palin, Christie, Carson, Perry, Quayle, Cheney and Duke) then Donald is right up your alley and heaven help us!

---

[77]Schwartz, Ian. Trump: "'They Can Chop Off Heads, We Can't Waterboard'"; Should 'Torture' Arrested Paris Terrorist." Real Clear Politics, 3/22/16.

Chapter 11: Nicknames

Donald knows he's an attraction. Right from the beginning of his campaign in the middle of 2015, his reputation as a tough guy who's in control made people sit up and pay attention. At the beginning there were seventeen candidates for the Republican Presidential nomination. How does one get noticed?

When the winnowing process began, though Donald had perhaps the best name recognition, Jeb Bush was the favorite among Republicans. Donald is used to street fights. Take a look at the structure of his hit show, "The Apprentice" (and "The Celebrity Apprentice"). Sixteen to eighteen people compete for the prize (is it just coincidental that there were seventeen candidates in the Republican Presidential scrum?). Each week, one of the show's competitors is cut by Donald, using his now famous trademark, "You're fired!" Am I crazy, or does he usually seem to enjoy this part of the show? "It is notable that Trump was shown to have the ultimate discretion in running the boardroom and at times he would disregard the typical format of the show, including firing multiple candidates in one week, firing candidates before the final stage, and bringing candidates back into the final stage who were not chosen by the project manager."[78] In other words, Donald did whatever he wanted to in Donaldworld. And since he was the ultimate boss, who was going to oppose him?

It's not surprising that, given his dictatorial style in both business and television, that Donald would feel comfortable getting down in the gutter to win this kind of a political contest. And, no one else in the group, with the

---

[78] wikipedia

possible exception of Chris Christie was familiar or comfortable with street fighting. And Christie, already having a reputation as a bully, never gained enough traction in the polls to be a factor in the race.

Donald, seeing Bush as his biggest competition, came up with a phrase (on 8/19/15) that stuck: "low energy." Unfortunately for Bush, it was a two word description of the way he came across at his campaign stops and in the debates. Though Bush was qualified and knowledgable and generally considered a decent man, these quickly became irrelevant. Jeb was eventually cooked or, to borrow a term, was "fired!" from the competition though he himself wouldn't know it for months.

Steeled by success, and probably proud of his emasculation of Bush, Donald continued to throw out nicknames and/or insults. If they seemed to work, he continued along that path. If they didn't stick, he'd find another approach. He insulted Carly Fiorina's looks ("Look at that face!" Would anyone vote for that? Can you imagine that, the face of our next president?!"). That got a lot of criticism so he abandoned that line of attack. He settled on "Lyin' Ted" and "Little Marco" both of which stuck, at least among his supporters. But there was a grain of truth in each of those insults. Fiorina was wooden and robotic in her presentation, Cruz came across as a manipulator that had no allies in Congress, and Rubio seemed as if he had some growing up to do.

There were also times when Donald got a lot of pushback, and though he never apologized for his rudeness or bad taste, he did walk them back a bit or deny his words. He attacked John McCain, who most Americans consider a war hero saying, "He's not a war hero," He was a war hero because he was captured? I like people who weren't captured."[79] In February of 2016, Donald denied the insult. "Well, it just shows you how they lie. Number one, I never called John McCain a loser, as you know. I like John McCain, I supported John McCain. I said he was a hero because he got caught, which is true, to a certain extent."[80] Now it's true that Donald didn't call McCain a loser at that time (he had previously), but by focusing on the word "loser" rather than "he's not a hero" he could claim to be the truthteller.

Then there was the Megyn Kelly fracas. Kelly asked Donald,

> "Mr. Trump, one of the things people love about you is you speak your mind and you don't use a politician's filter. However, that is not without its downsides, in particular, when it comes to women. You've called women you don't like 'fat pigs,' 'dogs,' 'slobs' and 'disgusting animals.' ...
>
> Your Twitter account has several disparaging comments about women's looks. You once told a contestant on 'Celebrity Apprentice' it would be a pretty picture to see her on her knees. Does that sound to you like the temperament of a man we should elect as president, and how will you answer the charge from Hillary Clinton, who was likely to be the Democratic

---

[79] Schreckinger, Ben. "Trump attacks McCain: 'I like people who weren't captured'." politico.com, 7/18/15.

[80] Haberman, Maggie. "Donald Trump Denies Saying What He Said About John McCain." FirstDraft, New York Times, 2/8/16.

nominee, that you are part of the war on women?"[81]

Donald then played hardball in his typical fashion, tweeting all sorts of insults at Kelly, feuding with Roger Ailes of FOX news (who backed Kelly) and saying that he would boycott the network. This didn't work for either side. Donald was deprived of an audience likely to support him and FOX was deprived of the viewers that Donald brought to the network. After some behind the scenes machinations a truce was called; Kelly gave Donald a "softball" interview during which they made nice and Donald returned to FOX. Many saw this as a capitulation on the part of FOX.[82]

The interesting thing about this interchange is that Kelly was one of the first people to hold Donald accountable for what he said, in this case about women. What ensued was Donald hitting back twice as hard and winning in the end. The net effect proved to Donald that scurrilous attacks worked for him and, as important, that responding to scurrilous attacks did not pay for the attacker. Once burned, twice shy.

Another ridiculous attack that Donald got away with through denial involved a disabled reporter from the New York Times. At a rally in South Carolina, Donald mocked the reporter by flailing his own arms in the air and imitating a stuttering voice. Every medium came down hard on Donald, but he simply denied ever having met the reporter

---

[81] Blake, Aaron. "Here are the Megyn Kelly questions that Donald Trump is still sore about." Washington Post, 1/26/16.

[82] Boehlert, Eric. "How Megyn Kelly's Softball Interview With Trump Signaled Fox News' Complete Surrender." alternet.org, 5/27/16.

(which was a lie) and said he never mocked him (which is obvious on the video).[83]

> "And I said, the reporter -- I didn't know who the reporter was, but I said a reporter was groveling. I'm just imitating a reporter. I was not imitating -- I would never -- who would ever do that? If somebody had a disability who would mock a disability? I would never -- I'm a smart person. I went to the Wharton School of Finance, like smart, good student, my uncle, professor at MIT, and all that stuff, who would ever mock somebody, especially in you're running for office? I would never do that."[84]

The interesting thing here is that no one called him a liar. Perhaps the news outlets feared being attacked and boycotted, as did FOX. Perhaps as a general principle networks feel that they need to be dispassionate about the content of the message; in other words, just report what was said and leave off any opinions. It is certain that no individual newscaster or reporter has much incentive to challenge Donald's veracity or style after what happened to Megyn Kelly and the disabled Times reporter.

Additionally, and this is the genius of Donald, he switches the attack to another subject or person on the next day, so that yesterday's outrageous comment is supplanted by today's. The networks, knowing that viewers eat this stuff up, are eager to move on to the new raw meat that Donald throws out there. It's a combination of rubbernecking at accidents on the side of the road and that

---

[83] CNN News Video, 11/26/15.

[84] Taken from a CNN interview by Jake Tapper, 11/26/15.

most people not being able to believe how outrageous Donald's words or actions can be.

It's also interesting that some of those rivals and public officials that Donald attacked most viciously, have jumped on the bandwagon since he locked up the nomination. This is what he said about Dr. Ben Carson who was rising in the polls before the Iowa caucuses, thus presenting a threat…

> "A few hours after claiming that Republican rival Ben Carson has an incurable 'pathological temper' and comparing it to something else he says is incurable — 'child molesting' — Trump escalated the battle, devoting over ten minutes of his rally to attacking Carson's personal narrative…" [Notice that Donald somehow equates having a pathological temper with child molesting. Where he got this from only Donald knows.]
>
> 'I said that if you're a child molester, a sick puppy, a child molester, there's no cure for that - there's only one cure and we don't want to talk about that cure, that's the ultimate cure. No there's two, there's death and the other thing. But if you're a child molester, there's no cure, they can't stop you. Pathological, there's no cure.'
>
> [Then Donald turns his attention to the story Carson told in his memoir…] 'I have a belt. If someone hits, you not going in, it moves this way, it moves that way, he hit the belt buckle,'

he said as he showed his belt buckle. Trump even asked the crowd if they wanted to 'try it' on him because 'believe me, it ain't going to work.'

Trump's story continued: 'And he plunged it into the belt and amazingly the belt stayed totally flat and the knife broke.' Trump then plunged a rhetorical knife of his own to the Iowa crowd: 'How stupid are the people of Iowa? How stupid are the people of the country to believe this crap?'[85]

Lo and behold, Donald began kissing up to Carson. In the beginning of March, after Carson suspended his campaign, he endorsed Donald, saying that they had "buried the hatchet" and that Donald's slurs were "just politics." Apparently Carson was wined and dined at a Donald-resort, Donald let Carson see his charming side (which [86]does exist) and offered him some sort of role in his Presidency, which Carson first said and then retracted. So not only do politicians prevaricate, but they also can be bought.

Recently, Donald may have met his match in Elizabeth Warren, Democrat Senator from Massachusetts. Warren is no milquetoast. When she criticized him on the stump, Donald responded by referring to her as "goofy" and "the Indian," and later "Pocahontas." This refers to Warren's stating that she recalls family members discussing their Cherokee heritage, which was never proven and can't

---

[85] Vitali, Ali. "Donald Trump Goes Off on Ben Carson's 'Pathological Temper'." nbcnews.com, 11/13/15.

[86] Rappeport, Alan. "Elizabeth Warren Turns Up the Anti-Donald Trump Volume." New York Times, 5/25/16.

be disproven. His attack might be seen as amusing, if it weren't so racist. Many prominent Republicans slammed him for this attack.[87]

Not shrinking at all from the fight, Warren called Donald "…a man who cares about no one but himself. A small, insecure money-grubber who doesn't care who gets hurt so long as he makes a profit off it… …"Donald Trump is worried about helping poor little Wall Street?" Ms. Warren said. "Let me find the world's smallest violin to play a sad, sad song."

A few weeks later, referring to Donald's attack on Judge Curiel, "'Trump is picking on someone who is ethically bound not to defend himself – exactly what you'd expect from a thin-skinned, racist bully,' Warren said, defending Judge Curiel against Trump Thursday night.

Noting that Trump has said Judge Curiel should be ashamed of himself Warren said it is Trump who should be ashamed and called the presumptive GOP nominee 'a total disgrace.'

'No, Donald – you should be ashamed of yourself, ashamed,' Warren said. 'Ashamed for using the megaphone of a Presidential campaign to attack a judge's character and integrity simply because you think you have some God-given right to steal people's money and get away with it. You shame yourself and you shame this great country.'

'Race-baiting a judge who spent years defending America from the terror of murderers and drug traffickers simply because long ago his family came to America from

---

[87] Gold, Matea, Demirjian, Haroun & DeBonis, Mike. "Trump's 'Pocahontas' attack leaves fellow Republicans squirming (again)." Washington Post, 6/10/16.

somewhere else. You, Donald Trump, are a total disgrace,' she said."[88]

If one notices, Donald's criticisms of Warren as "goofy" and falsely claiming Native American status is just name calling. Warren, though not timid in response, at least includes content in her barbs, involving race baiting and being a profiteer. It seems that Warren relishes the role of attack dog, and will be a funnel for all the Democrat talking points for the rest of the campaign. Donald, you have finally found your match.

Republicans too, seem to be standing up to Donald. Mitt Romney said, "Trump appeals 'to racism, xenophobia, misogyny, violence. I just can't do that,' Romney said, calling it 'trickle down racism.'" Notice that Romney's criticisms had content, implying general issues of racism, fear of the other, dislike of women and fomenting violence.

Predictably Donald's response was content free, consisting of calling Romney names, as one would in a fifth grade schoolyard argument. "'I watched this poor sad Mitt Romney this morning. He suffers from misogynist. I don't think he knows what misogynist is,' Trump told the crowd… [It is likely that Donald was making a joke here, but unlikely that many in his audience knew that.]

…Trump added: 'But then when I heard he was gonna run again and I was thinking about running, I let him know. I said the guys a stone cold loser, he choked and when you're a choker, you can never give a choker a second change. It's too important. A choker is a choker.'"[89]

Pure unmitigated name-calling.

---

[88] Phelps, Jordyn. "Vice President Joe Biden, Elizabeth Warren Tear Into Trump." abcnews.go.com, 6/9/16.

[89] Caldwell, Leigh Ann. "Mitt Romney Reflects on How Donald Trump's Comments Are 'Breaking My Heart'." nbcnews.com, 6/12/16.

Chapter 12: Convenient fantasies (Policies?)

Does Donald have actual policies? I mean, does he have plans to solve actual problems that face our nation both at home and abroad? In a way he does, or at least *says* he does. On closer inspection, not much of what he says he will do is achievable, or is within existing laws or is under the purview of the Executive Branch.

> "Looking at Donald's plan to deal with ISIS, he has 'vowed to "bomb the hell out of" oil fields controlled by the terror group. The problem with that, military analysts have said, is that most of the oil field controlled by ISIS are in Syria, not Iraq."
>
> 'We're going to have so much money,' Trump declared in his interview with…' [As if not only will be able to bomb their oil fields, but after we put out the flames and mine the oil, we'll be able to sell it at a profit. Sure…]
>
> "Then-Army Chief of Staff Ray Odierno suggested that there are limits to military power in responding to Trump's plan, particularly in the long-term political and economic consequences of destroying the livelihoods of "Iraqi civilians without cutting off the terror group's cash flow. 'It's about sustainable outcome. And the problem we've had is, we've had outcomes, but they've been only short-term outcomes because we haven't

looked at, we haven't properly looked at, the political and economic sides of this. It's got to be all three that come together. And if you don't do that, it's not going to solve the problem,' he said"[90]

Then Donald would play hardball with Mexico; he says, with no repercussions. "Describing how he would negotiate with the CEO of an American car company that wanted to relocate to or build a manufacturing plant in Mexico, Trump had an imagined conversation during his June 16 announcement. 'I would call up the head of Ford, who I know,' Trump said, going on to say that he would say, 'Congratulations. That's the good news. Let me give you the bad news. Every car and every truck and every part manufactured in this plant that comes across the border, we're going to charge you a 35-percent tax, and that tax is going to be paid simultaneously with the transaction, and that's it.' That would, as the Washington Post's initial fact check stated, seem to violate the North America Free Trade Agreement (a treaty that Trump has openly disdained). It also does not take into account the fact that only Congress could establish separate tax rates under the Constitution." [Details, details.]

That's not to mention the wall that Donald would build, paid for by Mexico, after the way he spoke about the Mexican people. Apparently, Donald did his research by talking to, we're sure, many many border guards. Well then, his conclusion has to be valid, no?

And then, after taxing anything made in Mexico at the rate of 35%, insulting the Mexican people and making

---

[90] Gass, Nick. "Donald Trump's 11 worst foreign policy gaffes." politico.com, 9/4/15.

them pay for a wall that Donald wants built, then and only then, will he send 11 million of them back across the border. To be fair, he will allow some of the good ones to come back. So yes, Donald does have a policy for dealing with Mexico!

Donald also has said he wants to repeal and replace Obamacare. Okay, but how would he do it. The Republican House of Representatives has tried repeal it approximately 50 times with no success. The probable reason for this is that no one has come up with another plan that is both better and viable. If we assume that there are many bright minds in the House of Representatives, it is likely that there is no obvious plan that is better. The only thing that remains is to tweak the existing rules to streamline the program.

Donald did come out with a plan, but the things he says are full of contradictions. He wants to repeal the ACA, but won't let anyone "die in the streets" if they have no coverage. He wants to prevent the insurance companies from denying coverage to anyone with preexisting conditions, but in the same breath rails against the individual mandate. Without the latter, only sick people would sign up for health care and the system would be unaffordable. Again, he has a policy, but it won't work.

Sometimes his stances on issues change so frequently that one has to laugh. About waterboarding and other forms of torture he has said, that the military will obey him and carry out illegal orders (3/3/16). Then, he said the military shouldn't have to do anything illegal (3/4/16). Now he favors not breaking any laws (such as the Geneva convention), but changing them to make some forms of torture, like waterboarding, legal.[91]

By the way, did you know that "Americans use guns to defend themselves against violent crime more than a million times a year," said Trump."[92] Apparently Donald made this one up, to fit the situation. The statement has been frequently proven false. Then there was his assertion that Hillary wants to abolish the Second Amendment. These are the types of "facts" that Donald bases his gun policies on.

Finally, one would think that since Donald is a great businessman, his economic and fiscal policies would be well-formed and well-received. Apparently, not so. "…economists say Trump is most vulnerable to attacks that his tax plan would deliver massive benefits to the wealthiest Americans. According to the Tax Policy Center, Trump's tax plan would reduce federal revenue by $9.5 trillion over the next decade. It would also provide an average $1.3 million tax cut for the top 0.1 percent of earners, the Tax Policy Center found. The Trump campaign has disputed these findings."[93]

His goal of deporting 11 million immigrants is seen as disastrous to the economy, as is his desire to place high import tariffs on imports. Mass deportation is predicted to lead to a depression in our economy, and tariffs would end up being a tax on U.S. consumers, since prices for foreign

---

[91] Timm, Jane C. "A Full List of Donald Trump's Rapidly Changing Policy Positions." nbcnews.com, 3/30/16.

[92] Collins, Gail. "Meet Deadeye Donald." New York Times Op-Ed, 5/20/16.

[93] White, Ben. "Economists savage Trump's economic agenda." politico.com, 1/11/16.

goods would rise dramatically. "Part of the problem with Trump, economists say, is the rhetoric that informs the real estate billionaire's policies and thrills his supporters, is not based on economic reality."[94]

---

[94] ibid

Chapter 13: The Intimidator

Listening to Jake Tapper's interview of Donald which aired on CNN on Sunday June 5, 2016, many of Donald's "tricks" were on display.

When Tapper asked questions Donald nodded his head agreeably. Donald rarely got anywhere near answering a question, however. When Tapper tried to insert a follow up such as, "What does that have to do with…", Donald would interrupt him and go off on a tangent, usually involving how great a businessman he was. Tapper was interrupted or over-talked on just about every follow up question.

Donald would concede nothing, even the fact that Clinton gave a speech that was tough on him. He maintained that it was prepared by others and read off a teleprompter by her, implying that it didn't count as a speech.

Responding to Clinton's accusation that he has "thin skin" Donald told Tapper how thick his skin is, how strong and in control his temperament is. This wasn't so bad, except he quickly segued into bragging about how great a businessman he was and how successful he had become. When Tapper asked, "What does this have to do with temperament," Donald again swerved, talking about how weak and ineffective our leadership is and how other countries have taken total advantage of us.

Hardly skipping a beat, Donald continued to say, "She mentions that I'll bring us into war. She's the one who brought us into Iraq, she raised her hand. She didn't know what the hell she was doing. I said I don't want to go into Iraq. I said it would destabilize the Middle East. I was 100% right. When Tapper pointed out that the first time he is on record saying we don't belong in Iraq, it was *a year after the invasion* (2004), Donald was not deterred. He repeated himself, saying, "I think there is evidence, I haven't been asked that question before [yeah right!], there are articles and I'll see if I can get it," promising to produce evidence that showed he was against the war before it started, though it's quite clear that if they existed, they would've seen the light of day well before this interview.

Changing the subject again, Donald went off into a jag about how the war destabilized the Middle East and that he warned us it would happen and then veered off on a tangent about Iran taking over the middle east.

Tapper then asked for a response to Clinton's accusation that Trump was racially biased for attacking the credibility of the "Mexican" judge (he was born in Indiana to parents of Mexican descent) who was presiding over a suit against Trump University. His defense, which he repeated at least three times, was that since he was building a wall between the U.S. and Mexico, anyone of Mexican descent couldn't be impartial. At times he went on off on rants about Clinton's e-mails (which he said gave her no right to comment and that she should be in jail), about how many people loved his Trump U. courses, about describing the details of his side of the legal case, and how he would do well with Hispanic voters because he was going to create jobs. Tapper kept returning to the race issue, but Donald would not admit that his comment was racist, instead repeating, "I'm building a wall. He's a Mexican."

Tapper looked very frustrated for much of the twenty minutes of the interview that was aired. Donald is a tough customer. Even the body language was telling. Tapper sat back in his chair, as if on defense, and Donald leaned forward, ready for action.

One thing Donald did and does consistently is not respect the boundaries of a conversation. It was apparent in the debates. Whenever he was being addressed by a rival he would start talking over the other person and not stop even though it was on the other candidate's time. He would not let any comment about him go unchallenged or unqualified. If he had nothing relevant to say, he would say something derogatory about the other person.

In the above interview, Donald frequently interrupted Tapper's follow-up question that he was trying to avoid. He would change the subject and go off sideways to attack either Hillary or some other foil, such as the judge in the Trump U. case. His comments and diatribes were almost always irrelevant to the topic that Tapper raised. And Tapper didn't, couldn't or wouldn't call him on it.

Which brings us to the intimidation factor, which is perhaps the most important of Donald's tricks. Who has the power to oppose him? In the debates, anyone who did was mocked and eviscerated by Donald, AND THE MODERATORS DID NOTHING! The targets of his attacks tried to protest on occasion, but since the others are relatively civil people, in effect they DID NOTHING! The only way things might have been different was if the network holding the debate gave the moderators the power to turn off the microphone of the insulter or to chastise him in some other way. But the networks DID NOTHING!

In the above interview, the only way Tapper could've pressed Donald to stay on topic and answer the question and not interrupt, was if his network, CNN, gave him the power to stop the interview, or to say things such as "Donald, that is irrelevant" or "Answer the question please" or "Please don't interrupt me" or, "That is a lie!" But the networks DIDN'T AND WON'T!

When in press conferences, how is a reporter who is trying to press Donald or ask him an uncomfortable question supposed to react when Donald "calls him out" and insults him for doing his job? Remember, every reporter's job *and* whole career are on the line. The only way that will happen is if the reporter walks out of the press conference and, by agreement, other reporters follow suit. In order for that to happen, the parent companies, newspapers or TV networks would have to be in agreement that they were not going to be bullied. BUT THEY HAVEN'T AND PROBABLY WON'T!

Ironically, Donald can intimidate without even trying and without intention. It's built into our political system. There are many Republicans who find Donald's beliefs and tactics odious, but can't or won't come out and stand up to him, except for minor statements of disagreement with this or that. Why? Because they are concerned about down-ballot issues. If a Republican Senator is running for re-election in 2016 he or she will be afraid that coming out strong against Donald will lose them votes and subsequently the election. Most centrist Republicans do not want Donald to be there standard bearer, but it's too late to do anything about that now, as of June, 2016. The quandary is if the party bigwigs denounce him, will they end up sabotaging each and every down ballot race? Not wanting to lose the Senate and House along with the Presidency, they stay relatively mum. SO WHO IS GOING TO SAY THAT THE EMPEROR IS WEARING NO CLOTHES?

The only way Donald will stop his over-talking, interrupting, changing the subject, telling lies, going off on tangents and being irrelevant is if someone makes him stop. And no one, so far anyway, has found that it was in their best interest to do so. I hate the analogy between Donald and the Hitler's Third Reich, but doesn't this all sound like the appeasement policy of Neville Chamberlain in Britain in the 1930s?[95]

---

[95] wikipedia. "Chamberlain is best known for his appeasement foreign policy, and in particular for his signing of the Munich Agreement in 1938, conceding the German-speaking Sudetenland region of Czechoslovakia to Germany."

Chapter 14: This Ain't Beanbag

Mike Barnicle of MSNBC's "Morning Joe" made an interesting observation on Friday, June 3, 2016. After watching President Obama indirectly criticize Donald for his racial and ethnic biases, saying that America doesn't stand for that, Barnicle said something to the effect of, "You've got one guy with dignity and gravitas, and another guy on a podium in a red hat yelling…"

What are the possible outcomes of the November, 2016 election? If Donald loses the election by a wide margin, society will not be overly changed. Let's assume 60-40, which would approximate the popular vote split for what are considered landslide victories achieved by Warren Harding in 1920,, F.D.R. in 1936, Lyndon Johnson in 1964, Richard Nixon in 1972 and Ronald Reagan in 1984.[96] If this happens, Donald along with his brand of politics will probably exit the public stage. Supporters of his will be scorned and the more moderate wing of the Republican party, now represented by Paul Ryan and Mitch McConnell, may again achieve ascendance. Politics as usual, hopefully with some lessons learned.

If he loses in a close election, but gets 45% or more of the popular vote, his type of politics and his tactics may remain operative in future election cycles and his influence will continue to make us a more contentious and rude society. As long as he loses, his "policies" will have little staying power since they are virtually unknown and changeable and not an important part of his "schtick." The

---

[96] Ebersole, Phil. "Five great 20th century Presidential landslides." philebersole.wordpress.com (blog), 2/18/11.

Paul Ryan wing of the party will still have to struggle against acolytes of Donald but he, being around 74 the next time around, may be much less of a factor. His imprint will be mostly on the street fighting nature of the campaign process.

It's only if Donald wins, that our society as we know it will be put at risk. For example, if elected, we will get a President with a diagnosed mental disorder: narcissistic personality disorder. (The reader might want to google NPD.) This is not good news.

Despite being asked by advisors, interested potential allies and family members, it seems that Donald can't or won't tone it down. He *can't* because that's who he is and that's who he's always been. Personality disorders are often unrecognized by the afflicted party and hard to change even if recognized.

He *won't* because of the positive feedback he's gotten from his success in business and from the sycophants at his well-attended rallies, his victorious march through the primaries and his presumptive defeat of Hillary Clinton. If it ain't broke, don't fix it. It seems to have worked very well for him but will it work for us, the American people?

Donald is admittedly a marketing genius who employs sketchy tactics. He will do anything he needs to do to be heard and speak his mind. Calling from the White House to Morning Joe or other networks to sell his point of view is not beyond the question. And, of course, the talking heads will have to take his call. After all he's the President, now. If no one has found a good way to stand up to him before he won the Presidency, how will they do that after he's won?

If Senators, Congressmen, judges or anyone else disagrees with him, President Donald will find a way to silence them. He might refer to "having heard rumors" or will invoke a disproven conspiracy theory that will embarrass his enemies, or he might blame them for anything that has gone wrong in the country. If for example, there is another mass shooting, it will be Obama's fault for not doing something to prevent it while in office.

Or, he might call them "losers" or "incompetent" or "stupid" or "the worst." He might even use these appellations against judges that he doesn't agree with, or whose decisions go against what he thinks is correct. This may have serious consequences for the esteem in which the Supreme Court is held and for the stability of the balance of power among the three branches of government.

Donald will bully people that disagree with him. He will have his favorite scapegoats and make fun of them with unflattering and irrelevant nicknames. He will take joy in finding an achilles heel in a dissenter.

He will be loyal to his friends and demand loyalty in return from his appointees. They will be yes-men and yes-women and know that they cannot oppose him lest they hear the dreaded phrase, "You're fired!" He will surround himself with people who fawn over him, such as Chris Christie, Sarah Palin and Ben Carson, and then proceed to ignore their advice. Brighter more independent people will threaten him.

Our President is a great showman and will draw loyal crowds when he gives a speech that he will pander to and incite. Occasionally, there will be violence at these venues, especially if anyone in the crowd protests. In press conferences, reporters will soon learn not to hold him to what he says or has said or question the veracity of his assertions. He will still maintain that he loves every audience he addresses and that everyone and every group loves him. We will move in the direction of being a totalitarian society.

Donald will lie to us when he deems it necessary. After all, the ends justify the means, facts are fungible and the truth is just a matter of opinion. Donald will never back down from what he says and will never admit that he's been in error or that he's lied. He never has, and after winning the Presidency, why should he start now?

Foreign leaders will be wary of Donald, given his history of hostility and isolation on the international scene. He is likely to be rude and want one sided deals in his favor which will not go over well with trading partners in China, Mexico, Russia, Europe or anywhere else for that matter. They will likely be quite intolerant of Donald and our economy and reputation will suffer greatly as many countries discover new trading partners in Russia and Germany, and/or China cozies up to Mexico. Donald will, of course, blame the other countries or past administrations.

Donald, as President, will decide and change his policies without much reference to relevant information or history. He may make mistakes but they will be someone else's fault. Since he always has to win, he will project his feelings onto other people and groups and thus maintain that everyone is out to get him or is very interested in his lunch.

Donald will be the first President that many parents will be ashamed to hold up as an example to their children. After all, a leader that debases and demeans people, who cannot ever say that he is wrong or sorry, who tells lies and then denies ever saying what he said, and who is clearly out to feed his own ego, is nothing short of a horrible role model.

And in passing, Donald's Presidency will probably mean the end of society as we know it. Our country, and we that comprise its citizenry, will never be the same again.

Afterward

If the reader recalls, the Foreword to this book said that I had a tough time putting this book to bed because new and interesting factoids were coming out every day. The countervailing force was the need to get the book out while it was still relevant. Well, here's the latest and last input, provided by an article describing many of the things for which Donald has taken credit.[97] Here are some of them:

"That he got Hillary Clinton to say 'radical Islamism.'"

"That he was being congratulated for 'being right on Radical Islam' after the Orlando attack."

"That he 'broke the glass ceiling' for women."

"That he inspired Budweiser to rebrand its beer as 'America.'"

That he forced Ford's years-old decision to shift some truck production to Ohio"

"That he aided in the release of Americans in a prisoner swap with Iran."

"That he caused planned federal raids on undocumented immigrants."

---

[97] Krieg, Gregory. "An incomplete list of all the things Donald Trump has taken credit for." cnn.com, 6/13/16.

"That he won the 2012 GOP primary in Nevada for Mitt Romney."

Now if this is not the mark of a narcissist, I'm not sure what is. Every good thing that happens while Donald is on the planet, he had something to do with. And every bad thing that happens can be laid at the feet of an adversary.

As an exercise, I'd like the reader to imagine that Donald was a guy named Bob, but with Donald's personality. Bob lives in your neighborhood, has a regular job like you do and has a middle class income and lifestyle. Would you want to be friends with him? Would you want to attend social gatherings with him? Would you see through his braggadocio and lies? Would you tolerate his insults of you or other people you knew? Would you even want your kids playing with his kids over at his house? My guess is that you would stay as far away as possible from this nasty, hateful, reprehensible, contemptible person.

One last thought. As a psychologist I often see families, some of whom function better than others. One thing that is important to every member is that they can trust what another member says. If a boy says that he did his homework, a parent won't be pleased to find out that he didn't do it. If a girl says she'll be at Janie's house, a parent won't be pleased if it is found out later that she was at her boyfriend's house. If a divorced Dad says he'll pick up the kids on Sunday morning and doesn't show, the kids will lose trust in him. Telling the truth is important and is the basis for feeling loved. If a divorced Dad badmouths his ex- (or vice versa), the kids will be caught in the middle and suffer as a result.

Now look at Donald's family. I will assume that his family members feel loved by Donald and that they are all bright women and men. If they are bright, they have to know that what their father is selling is snake oil. They have to know that he lies and is rude and is hurtful to others, be it through name calling or business deals that lose millions of dollars for others while enriching their father.

It is easy to envision them being caught in a web of opposing motivations. They certainly love him as their father and they must be, to some extent, brainwashed by hearing his side of the story day after day. They also likely know the tactics that their father uses (including name calling and lying) are wrong but believe that the ends justify the means. And, just like all the others, they are likely to be intimidated to the point where they dare not oppose him. Each time I see him giving a speech with his beautiful and dutiful wife and children standing behind him, with fixed "Stepford Wives" smiles on their faces, I wonder what's going on in their heads.

www.ingramcontent.com/pod-product-compliance
Lightning Source LLC
Chambersburg PA
CBHW020016050426
42450CB00005B/495